REFUGEES

by Holly Duhig

BookLife PUBLISHING

©2018
BookLife Publishing
King's Lynn
Norfolk PE30 4LS

A catalogue record for this book is available from the British Library.

ISBN: 978-1-78637-429-5

Written by:
Holly Duhig

Edited by:
Kirsty Holmes

Designed by:
Dan Scase

APPROVED

PHOTO CREDITS

CONTENTS

Words that look like **THIS** are explained in the glossary on page 31.

WHO ARE REFUGEES?

A refugee is someone who has no choice but to leave their home country and is unable to return there because it is too dangerous. Refugees have to travel to other countries and apply for asylum there. Asylum is a word that means safety and protection. A refugee can apply for asylum, which means that they are asking a country's government for protection. A person waiting to be granted asylum is called an asylum seeker. Every person has the right to seek asylum.

REFUGEES IN KOS, GREECE

Refugees have to apply for asylum in the first safe country they reach.

When someone has been forced to leave their home but has not yet been granted asylum in another country, it is called being displaced.

Moving from one country to another with the intention of living there is called migrating, and people who do this are called migrants. All refugees are migrants because they are moving from one country to another, but not all migrants are refugees. Some people migrate out of choice because they want to live somewhere with more opportunities and better working or living conditions. By contrast, refugees have no choice but to migrate.

Moving into a country is called immigrating and moving out of a country is called emigrating.

REFUGEES WAIT TO REGISTER FOR ASYLUM IN PASSAU, GERMANY.

HOW DO PEOPLE BECOME REFUGEES?

55% OF REFUGEES COME FROM THESE THREE COUNTRIES:

SOUTH SUDAN
1.4 MILLION (M)

AFGHANISTAN
2.5 M

SYRIA
5.5 M

People become refugees for all sorts of reasons, such as war, natural disasters, extreme poverty, or the fear of **PERSECUTION**. When people are being mistreated in their own country because of things such as their race, religion, nationality or **POLITICAL** opinions, it might become too dangerous to live there and they may have to leave.

In 2017, over half the refugees in the world came from just three countries: Afghanistan, Syria and South Sudan. All these countries have been torn apart by war and are no longer safe places to live.

DAMASCUS, SYRIA, BEFORE AND AFTER THE CIVIL WAR

As well as war, many refugees are escaping persecution. The Rohingya people from Myanmar are discriminated against in their own country and are often victims of violence at the hands of their country's army and police force. Within the space of just two months in 2017, 603,000 refugees from Myanmar escaped to Bangladesh.

Throughout history, refugees have been people who were facing **DISCRIMINATION**.
During the 1930s and 1940s it became extremely dangerous for German-Jewish people to live in their home country. Before World War II broke out, thousands of them fled and became refugees.

The famous scientist Albert Einstein was a Jewish refugee from Germany who migrated to the USA.

In South Sudan the ongoing civil war and dry weather have caused a devastating **FAMINE** that has affected around 4.9 million people. Many people from South Sudan have left their families in an attempt to find work in other countries where they can earn money to send back to their family. This could be the difference between life and starvation. Sometimes male members of the family have no choice but to join the army so they can earn money. However, often they don't earn enough or they die in the conflict.

In the 1800s, thousands of Irish refugees fled to the United States and Canada due to famine. Out of 100,000 refugees who left, 30,000 died on the journey or shortly after.

Water is being **RATIONED** in this refugee camp in South Sudan.

GUATEMALA

HONDURAS

EL SALVADOR

People might also become refugees because they are attempting to escape violence in the country they live in. Many people from countries in Central America such as Guatemala, El Salvador and Honduras are seeking asylum due to horrific violence. Criminal groups and gangs make these places very unsafe to live. Families, especially women and children, are on the run and looking for a safe place to live, work and go to school. Many children are forced to make the journey alone and risk being targeted or even **RECRUITED** by gangs.

In 2016, 388,000 people fled this region of Central America.

San Salvador, the capital city of El Salvador, is one of the most violent cities in the world.

CASE STUDY: SYRIA

Problems began in Syria in early 2011, when Syrian people began to **PROTEST** against the actions of the Syrian president, Bashar al-Assad. By the middle of 2011, the protesters had armed themselves for protection and, as the violence increased, a civil war started.

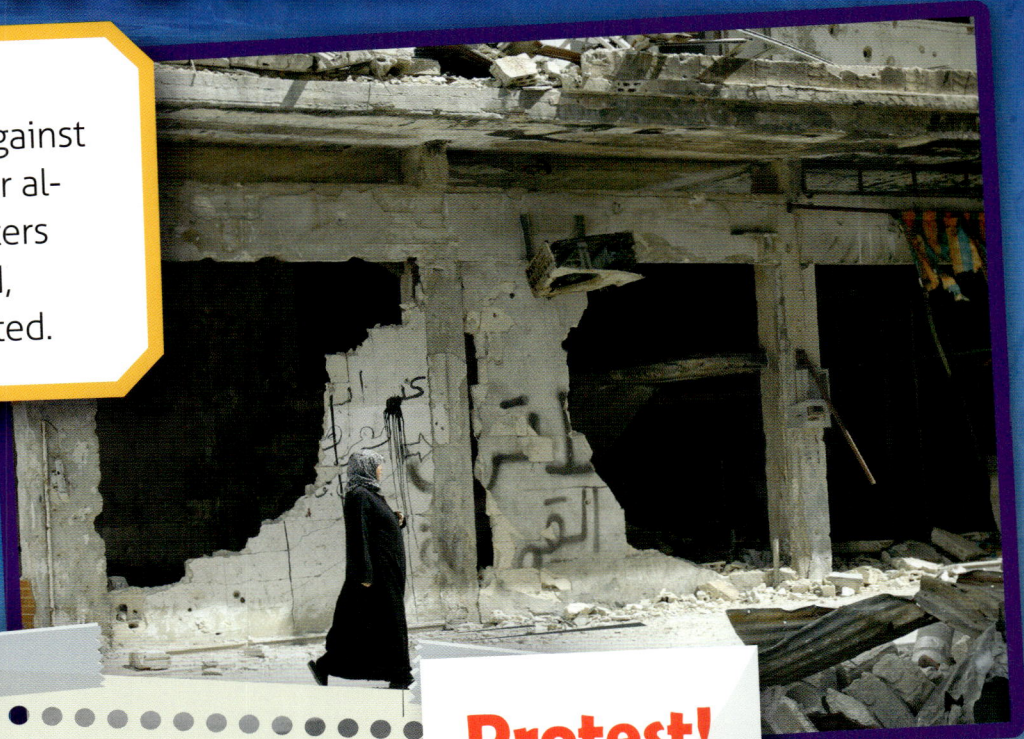

PRESIDENT ASSAD

The civil war between those who support President Assad and those who do not has become increasingly violent. Between 2011 and 2014, 191,000 people were killed.

Protest!

Since the war began, other groups (including the so-called Islamic State) have become involved in the fighting and have claimed control of large parts of the country.

When someone is forced to flee their home but has not yet crossed a **BORDER** to a new country, it is called being internally displaced.

As a result of the violence across the country, more than four million people have fled from Syria and millions of others have been internally displaced. Buildings and homes have been destroyed and previously bustling towns and cities have been turned to rubble. Important buildings such as hospitals and schools have also been destroyed.

Many of the Syrian refugees have moved to nearby countries, such as Turkey, Jordan and Lebanon while others hope to seek safety in Europe.

11

REFUGEES AND THE LAW

In order to be granted refugee status and therefore be protected by refugee law, a person must meet certain CRITERIA. This includes being outside of their COUNTRY OF ORIGIN and having a fear of persecution if they return to that country.

If a person meets the criteria, it is illegal for them to be returned to the country in which their life would be at risk. This is called the principle of NON-REFOULEMENT.

International Refugee Law is mostly made up of the 1951 United Nations Convention Relating to the Status of Refugees and the 1967 Protocol Relating to the Status of Refugees. These laws were made to define what it means to be a refugee and to offer help and protection to refugees.

These refugees are lining up to register for asylum with the UN Refugee Agency.

In the UK, it is extremely difficult to be granted refugee status by law and many asylum applications are rejected. If an application is rejected, the person can appeal. If the appeal is unsuccessful, the person must leave the country.

Even when refugees are given refugee status in the UK, they aren't always given the **FINANCIAL SUPPORT** they need and they may not be given the right to work. This stops refugee families from being able to build a life for themselves in their new country.

In 2016, the UK refused asylum to 21,000 people.

THE JOURNEYS OF REFUGEES

When people migrate out of choice, they are usually able to plan their journey, take all of their belongings and leave the country in a safe way. Refugees usually have very little time to flee their country and are not able to take many of their belongings with them.

Sometimes, just one family member will make the dangerous journey to a new country and claim asylum. If they manage this, their family may be able to follow in a safer way.

These roads in Homs, Syria, have been destroyed.

Leaving the country that you have grown up in and where everyone speaks your language is very difficult. Many refugees want to return to their home country once it is safe to do so.

Refugees may face danger while travelling out of their country and, in the case of people fleeing a war, a lot of the INFRASTRUCTURE that allows people to travel, such as roads, airports or public transport, may be damaged or destroyed. This means that refugees often have to escape in ways that are dangerous and illegal.

Many refugees travel on foot, by boat and in the back of lorries, carrying their belongings with them. These journeys are extremely dangerous but are a refugee's only option.

It's important to remember that war or famine can affect everyone, and that refugees can be from all sorts of backgrounds. They can be rich or poor, young or old.

15

MIGRATION: BY BOAT

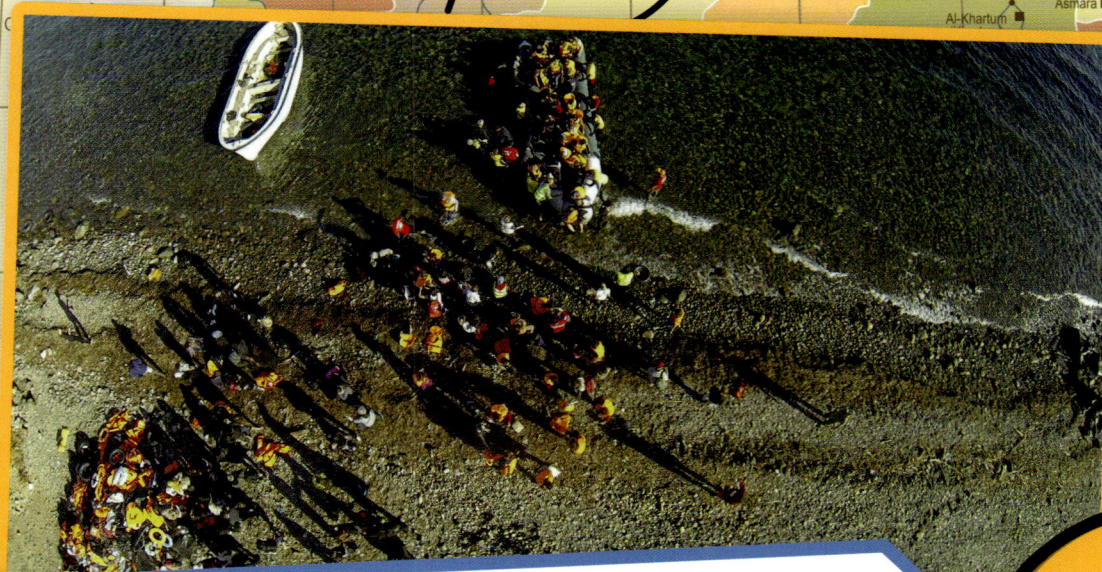

Refugees from Syria usually travel to Europe by travelling through Turkey. Some make this journey on foot, but it is very difficult to enter Europe this way, so many people travel by boat across the Mediterranean Sea. Refugees coming from countries in Africa often travel to North African countries like Libya and Tunisia and then cross the Mediterranean Sea to Europe.

Around 362,000 refugees risked their lives crossing the Mediterranean Sea in 2016.

KEY
— MAJOR LAND ROUTES
● MAIN MIGRATION HUBS
● COASTAL MIGRATION HUBS
····· FERRY ROUTES USED BY MIGRANTS

Some people illegally move people across borders. These people are called smugglers. One way they do this is by making refugees pay to cross the Mediterranean Sea in small boats called dinghies. These dinghies are not safety-checked and are often overcrowded, which means many of them break during the journey. Because of this, dinghies have broken down or capsized during the journey and thousands of refugees have drowned in the sea.

REFUGEE DEATHS IN MEDITERRANEAN SEA

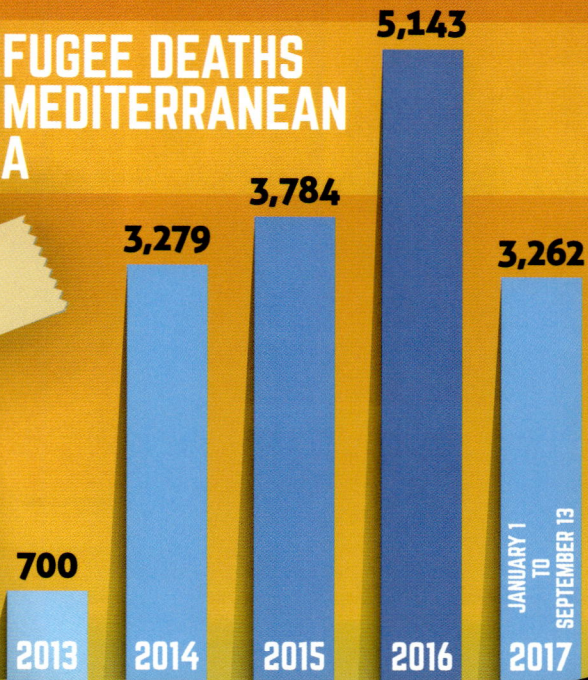

Year	Deaths
2013	700
2014	3,279
2015	3,784
2016	5,143
2017 (JANUARY 1 TO SEPTEMBER 13)	3,262

This graph shows how many refugees have died trying to cross the Mediterranean Sea in recent years.

Charities such as Médecins Sans Frontières (MSF) send out rescue boats to save people from drowning. In one year they rescued 21,603 refugees.

MIGRATION: ON FOOT AND BY LORRY

Many refugees have no choice but to undertake part of their journey to a new country on foot. People carry their belongings with them and their journey can be hundreds of kilometres long. Many families have older people and children with them who find the long journey even more difficult, especially when it is very hot or raining heavily. Parts of the journey on foot may be via dangerous routes, such as on busy roads or along train tracks.

Refugees travelling on foot often have to sleep on the streets.

Many refugees are attempting to enter countries such as the UK inside lorries. When traffic is at a standstill, refugees may try to climb inside the back of the lorries and hide there.

People-smugglers might illegally charge refugees large amounts of money for a space inside the container part of a lorry. However, travelling inside a lorry is extremely dangerous. The refugees have very little space and the containers are sealed so the people inside are cut off from fresh air.

In 2015, 71 people were found to have died inside a lorry in Austria. It is thought they were refugees from Syria.

In 2016, 15 people were rescued from the back of a lorry because a seven-year-old boy was able to send a text to a volunteer who had helped him in Calais.

REFUGEE CAMPS

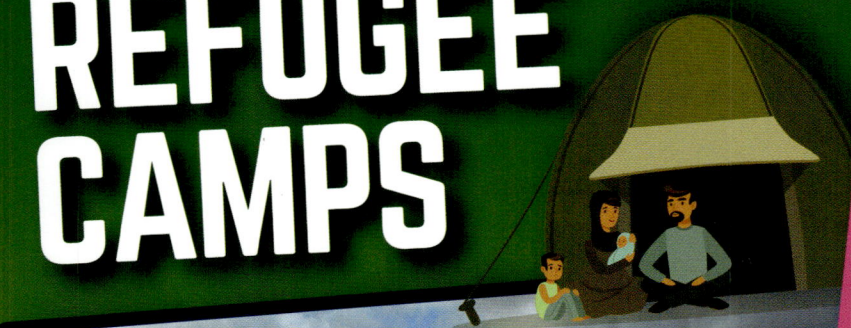

A refugee camp is a **TEMPORARY** place for refugees to live until they find a better home. As the camps are only intended to provide shelter for a short time, they are very basic. Unfortunately, people end up calling them home for a lot longer than they should have to. Refugee camps are very unpleasant places to live. They tend to be overcrowded and often there is not enough food and drink to go around. They also don't have enough important things such as toilets and showers.

Refugees are not allowed to leave refugee camps until they are given asylum. This can take a long time.

'THE JUNGLE', FRANCE

The Jungle in Calais, France, was one of the largest refugee camps in Europe before it was dismantled in 2016. People lived in tents and make-shift huts built from wood and plastic sheets. It was often cold and conditions were unclean, which meant many people became ill and suffered infections. At its highest, the **POPULATION** of the jungle was around 10,000 people, all of whom wanted to apply for asylum in France, the UK and other neighbouring countries in Europe.

Many people tried to escape the camp and enter the UK by walking the length of the channel railway tunnel.

Refugee camps are usually set up by a government or a charity, for example the Red Cross.

DADAAB, KENYA

Although in recent years more and more refugees have been seeking asylum in European countries, it is not only these countries that host refugees. One of the biggest refugee camps in the world is the Dadaab complex in Kenya with over 200,000 registered refugees and asylum seekers living there. Dadaab is actually made up of five separate camps: Dagahaley, Hagadera, Ifo, Ifo II and Kambioos. The camp was set up by the Kenyan government and the UNHCR (United Nations Refugee Agency) in the 1990s when people fled civil war in Somalia. Many of these refugees were never able to return and have grown up and had children in the Dadaab camps.

It can be very expensive for counties to host such large refugee camps. Kenya wants to work with Somalia to make it a safer country for people to return to.

BIDI BIDI, UGANDA

Uganda has one of the most **COMPASSIONATE** refugee policies in the world and they have welcomed thousands of refugees who are fleeing the civil war in South Sudan. Once you have refugee status in Uganda you are given land to build a home and the right to travel and work. However, Uganda now has the largest refugee camp in the world and the country is struggling to provide for the people living there.

Bidi Bidi refugee camp is in the Yumbe District shown here in red.

In March 2017, 2,800 refugees were migrating to Uganda every day.

Yumbe

Kaabong

Adjumani

Atiak

Kitgum

Arua

Pader

Kotido

Gulu

U G A N D A

Lira

Apac

Lake Kwania

Kaberamaido

Katakwi

Naka

Soroti

Lake Bisina

Lake Kyoga

Kumi

Sironko

Nakasongola

Pallisa

Mbale

Namasagali

Kamuli

Busembatia

Kiboga

Luwero

Iganga

Tororo

Kibale

Kayunga

Bundibugyo

Fort Portal

Kyenjojo

Mubende

Jinja

Bugiri

Busia

Mityana

Wakiso

Kampala

Mayuge

Kasese

Kamwenge

Mukono

Port Bell

Ntusi

Mpigi

Entebbe

Lake George

Sembabule

Masaka

Kalangala

Lyantonde

SESE ISLANDS

Lake Victoria

Bushenyi

Mbarara

Rakai

Rukungiri

Ntungamo

Kanungu

HOW CAN WE HELP REFUGEES?

Lots of people have different ideas about the best way to help refugees and so it is often talked about by governments and in the news. Some people feel that richer countries should help larger numbers of refugees. Other people feel their country does not have the money or **RESOURCES** to be able to help that many people, and that the number of refugees allowed to enter the country should be limited.

Each country has their own **POLICY** on refugees and therefore the number of people accepted is different for every country.

SWEDEN
32,215

ITALY
29,615

GERMANY
140, 910

FRANCE
20,630

NETHERLANDS
16,450

UK
13,905

This diagram shows how many people were given asylum in different countries in Europe. Germany helped the most refugees while the UK helped the least.

REFUGEES WELCOME

Many people think that governments of European countries should do more to help the refugees and allow more people to claim asylum. In the UK in 2015, around 100,000 people attended a **RALLY** in London to put pressure on the British government to allow more refugees to enter the UK. After the rally the government agreed to resettle 20,000 refugees by the year 2020.

Help 4 Refugee Children

REFUGEES WELCOME

No human is illegal

SAFE PASSAGE NOW!

People made signs with the words "refugees welcome" and "no human is illegal".

"It is not a crisis of the numbers of people coming, it is a crisis about the way the government is managing it." – Caroline Lucas, MP for the Green Party.

HOW DO PEOPLE FEEL ABOUT REFUGEES?

These volunteer lifeguards are helping people arriving in boats.

The charity organisation Save the Children launched a campaign in 2015 that raised £500,000 in its first 24 hours.

Many people want to help refugees and they do this in many ways. For example they might:

- Volunteer for or donate to charities that want to provide resources to refugees
- Go to rallies and put pressure on governments to provide more help
- VOTE for POLITICAL PARTIES who want to do more to help refugees

DONATE

Save the Children

This couple from Syria are learning English so they can live and work in New Zealand.

NO REFUGEES

Some people have a much more negative attitude towards refugees. They think that the people already living in a country should be the government's first **PRIORITY**. They think that if lots of refugees are welcomed into their country, then there will not be enough resources – like houses, jobs and money – to share around.

Many people and charities try to raise awareness of why this isn't true. Refugees don't want to just take things from the country they seek asylum in. They want to live and work there. By earning money and buying things refugees actually put money into a country's **ECONOMY**.

REFUGEES WELCOME

Many people think it shouldn't matter whether or not refugees cost safe countries money because it is the responsibility of these countries to end the suffering of refugees.

HOW DOES IT FEEL TO BE A REFUGEE?

People can usually only take what is most important to them.

For refugees, the journey to a new home can be extremely frightening. The journey itself is very dangerous and refugees may not have enough money with them to afford food and drink, or find shelter on the way. Refugees aren't necessarily poor but, because they have to leave their houses and belongings behind, they have very little while they are travelling. They may also have been separated from their friends and family, which is extremely distressing. Refugees may have loved ones who are still living in their home country and and they may not be able to find out if they are OK.

When refugees are given asylum in a new country, it can be very difficult to begin with. They may have gone to a country where people speak a different language and so they cannot understand what others are saying. This is called a language barrier.

Hello!
Salut!
Bonjour!
Hallo!
Ciao!
ПРИВЕТ!
مرحبا
नमस्ते
您好
Hi!
Hola!
Olá!
Salut!
Hi!

SUQ FESTIVAL, ITALY

The Suq Festival in Italy brings migrant families and locals together to celebrate their cultures.

In a new country, there may be different food, different clothes and different traditions. These are called **CULTURAL DIFFERENCES**. For many refugees these differences take some getting used to. However, as well as differences, there are lots of things that bring people from different cultures together.

REFUGEE CHARITIES

Luckily, charities, organisations and governments are working together to help refugees settle in new countries by building new lives and making new friends. Some of the charities that help refugees include:

Médecins Sans Frontières
British Red Cross
Save the Children
Refugee Action
Refugee Council
Safe Passage

Médecins Sans Frontières is French for 'Doctors without Borders'.

REFUGEES WELCOME

Safe Passage is a charity that creates safe and legal routes for refugees to travel through. They have helped 1,700 refugee children to arrive in the UK through the safe routes they have opened.

The British Red Cross gave over 80,870 people food and hygiene kits when they arrived by boat in Italy.

Ask an adult to help you learn more about these charities and what they do. You can even make a donation of clothes, money or food.

GLOSSARY

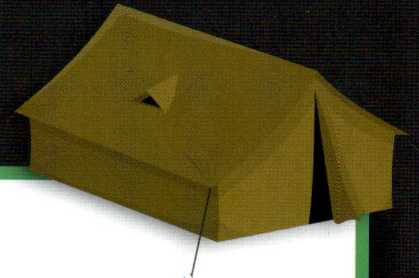

BORDER	the line separating two countries or areas
CIVIL WAR	fighting between different groups of people in the same country
COMPASSIONATE	feeling or showing sympathy and concern for others
COUNTRY OF ORIGIN	the country where someone is originally from
CRITERIA	standards by which something is judged
CULTURAL DIFFERENCES	the differences in the traditions, ideas and ways of life of certain groups of people
DISCRIMINATION	the unjust treatment of people based on arbitrary reasons, such as their race, gender, sex or age
ECONOMY	the way trade and money is controlled and used by a country or region
FAMINE	when large numbers of people do not have enough food
FINANCIAL SUPPORT	money given to support people when they arrive in a new country
INFRASTRUCTURE	the basic services, such as a power supply and roads, that a community needs in order to function
NON-REFOULEMENT	the practice of not forcing refugees or asylum seekers to return to a country in which they are likely to be in danger
PERSECUTION	cruel or unfair treatment based on race, religion or political beliefs
POLICY	a formal plan or set of rules about what to do in a particular situation
POLITICAL	associated with the activities of the government of a country
POLITICAL PARTIES	organised groups of people who have similar ideas about government
POPULATION	the number of people living in a place
PRIORITY	a thing that is regarded as more important than others
PROTEST	actions that express a disapproval of or objection to something, usually involving multiple people
RALLY	a mass meeting of people making a political protest or showing support for a cause
RATIONED	to allow each person to have only a fixed amount of something
RECRUITED	taken on or enrolled as a member or worker in an organization
RESOURCES	supplies of money, materials or people
TEMPORARY	only lasting for a short time
VOTE	to make a decision about who you want in your government

INDEX